Beaver

Janet Gurtler

Weigl

Published by Weigl Educational Publishers Limited
6325 10th Street SE
Calgary, Alberta T2H 2Z9
Website: www.weigl.com

Library and Archives Canada Cataloguing in Publication

Gurtler, Janet
          Beaver / Janet Gurtler.
(Canadian icons)
Includes index.
ISBN 978-1-77071-662-9 (bound).--ISBN 978-1-77071-668-1 (pbk.)
          1. Beaver (Emblem)--Juvenile literature.
2. Beavers--Canada--Juvenile literature.
I. Title. II. Series: Canadian icons

FC223.B4G88 2011   j929.90971   C2011-900807-6

Printed in the United States of America in North Mankato, Minnesota
1 2 3 4 5 6 7 8 9 0 15 14 13 12 11

052011
WEP37500

Editor: Heather Kissock
Art Director: Terry Paulhus

Weigl acknowledges Getty Images as the primary image supplier for this title.

Every reasonable effort has been made to trace ownership and to obtain permission to reprint copyright material. The publishers would be pleased to have any errors or omissions brought to their attention so that they may be corrected in subsequent printings.

We acknowledge the financial support of the Government of Canada through the Canada Book Fund for our publishing activities.

CONTENTS

What is a Beaver?

A beaver is an animal found throughout Canada. It has brown fur and a flat, wide tail. Beavers are a type of **rodent**. This means they have long front teeth that they use to nibble on food.

The beaver played an important role in Canada's past. Many people moved to Canada because of the beaver.

5

Beavers and Canada

In the 1600s and early 1700s, Europeans wore hats made from beaver fur. When explorers found beavers in Canada, they took the news back to Europe. Soon, English and French **fur traders** came to Canada to buy furs from **trappers**. The fur traders then sold the furs to hat makers in Europe.

Later, people began to wear hats made from silk. Beaver furs were no longer needed.

Beaver Features

The beaver is the largest rodent in Canada. It weighs between 15 and 35 kilograms. Beavers can be found in forests and streams across the country. They have many features that help them survive in these places. In nature, a beaver can live up to 24 years.

TAIL
A beaver uses its tail to steer through water. On land, the tail acts as a **prop** when the beaver is sitting.

BACK FEET
A beaver's back feet are **webbed**. They help the beaver swim.

FUR
The dark brown fur of a beaver is very thick. It is also **waterproof**.

FRONT PAWS
The beaver's front paws are like hands. The beaver uses them to hold and carry sticks and mud.

The Beaver Family

Beavers live in family groups. Families are made up of two parents and one to nine babies. Beaver babies are called kits.

The parents care for their kits together. Beavers are full grown when they are about two years old. They move away from home at this time.

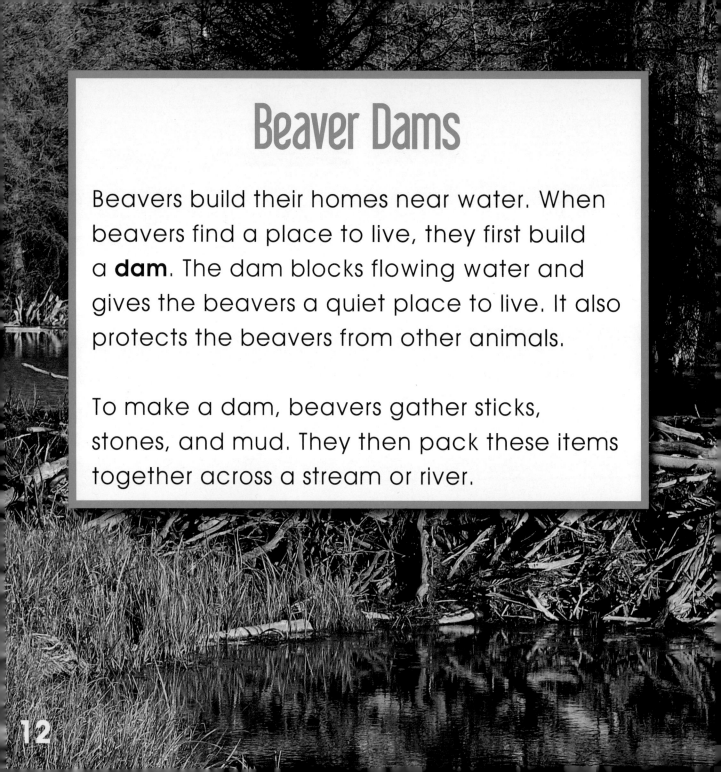

Beaver Dams

Beavers build their homes near water. When beavers find a place to live, they first build a **dam**. The dam blocks flowing water and gives the beavers a quiet place to live. It also protects the beavers from other animals.

To make a dam, beavers gather sticks, stones, and mud. They then pack these items together across a stream or river.

13

Staying at the Lodge

Once the dam is built, the beavers begin making their home. A beaver's home is called a lodge. Like dams, lodges are made of sticks, stones, and mud.

Beavers build their lodges on small islands and along riverbanks. The lodges have an underwater entrance that leads to a dry living area.

Favourite Foods

A beaver's favourite food is cambium. This is a soft layer under a tree's bark. Beavers use their sharp teeth to chew the bark from the trees. They especially like the cambium from aspen and willow trees.

Other foods eaten by beavers include roots, leaves, grasses, and water plants.

Going for a Swim

Beavers are strong swimmers. They can swim at speeds up to 8 kilometres per hour and stay underwater for up to 15 minutes. When a beaver is underwater, its nose and ears close to keep water out.

If a beaver senses danger, it slaps the water with its tail. This sends a warning to other beavers.

Special Beavers

In 1975, the beaver became Canada's **official** animal. The beaver was chosen because it played an important role in Canada's history.

Canada has honoured the beaver in many ways. In 1851, the beaver appeared on a Canadian postage stamp. Today, the beaver can be seen on Canadian nickels. There is also a special three-cent coin with a beaver on it.

Make a Beaver Mask

Supplies

a large
paper plate

brown paint

glue

scissors

pencil

one piece of
long string

black, brown, and white
construction paper

1. Cut out two holes in the plate for your eyes. Make sure the holes are big enough for you to see out.

2. Paint your paper plate brown, and let it dry completely. Make sure to put newspaper under the plate.

3. Using the scissors, cut out a round nose from the black construction paper. Glue it to the middle of the mask.

4. Cut two ears from the brown construction paper. Glue them to the back of the mask at the top.

5. Take the white construction paper, and cut out two long teeth. Glue the teeth to the front of the mask.

6. With the tip of the pencil, poke a tiny hole on each side of the plate. Tie each end of the string to the mask. Put your mask over your face. You are now a beaver.

Find Out More

To learn more about beavers, visit these websites.

Canadian Heritage—The Beaver
www.pch.gc.ca/pgm/
ceem-cced/symbl/o1-eng.cfm

Canadian Museum of Nature
http://nature.ca/notebooks/english/
beaver.htm

Hinterland Who's Who
www.hww.ca/hww2.asp?id=82

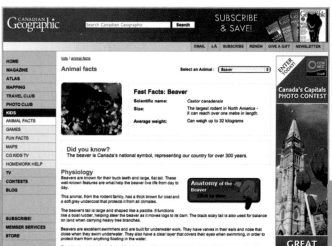

Canadian Geographic Kids
www.canadiangeographic.ca/
kids/animal-facts/beaver.asp

Glossary

dam: a wall built across a stream or river

fur traders: people who obtain animal furs and trade them for money or other items

official: approved for use

prop: an object used to hold something in a position

rodent: a type of animal with a pair of big front teeth that are used for chewing

trappers: people who trap animals for their fur

waterproof: does not let water pass through

webbed: having skin between the toes

Index

24